After an exciting visit to a natural history museum, David creates a fantasy with his imaginary dinosaur pet.

If a Dinosaur Came to Dinner

By Jane Belk Moncure

Illustrated by
Helen Endres

THE CHILD'S WORLD

ELGIN, ILLINOIS 60120

Library of Congress Cataloging in Publication Data

Moncure, Jane Belk.
 If a dinosaur came to dinner.

 (Creative dramatics)
 SUMMARY: A child imagines having a pet
dinosaur.
 [1. Play—Fiction. 2. Dinosaurs—Fiction.
3. Stories in rhyme] I. Endres, Helen.
II. Title. III. Series.
PZ8.3.M72If   [E]   77-12957
ISBN 0-89565-008-8

Distributed by Childrens Press, 1224 West Van Buren Street, Chicago,
Illinois 60607.

If a
Dinosaur
Came
to
Dinner

I know the dinosaurs died away
many years before today.

STEGOSAURUS

The ones in museums
are made of clay.

ALLOSAURUS

But imagine the fun
of playing with one,
a friendly, gentle one.

BRONTOSAURUS

If I had one
that was tall and tame,
I would teach him how
to play some games.
I would teach
football in fall . . .

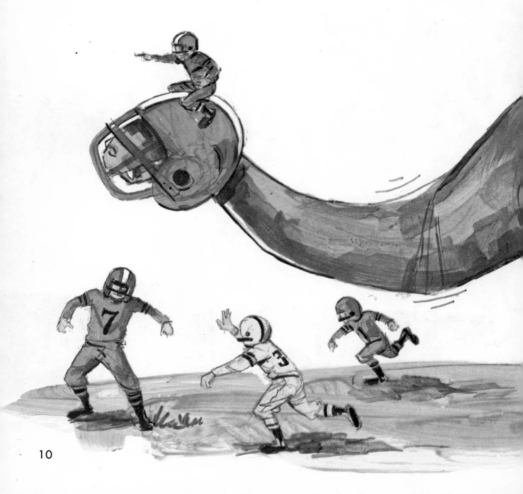

. . . baseball in spring.

He could learn most anything!

But he would be best
as a basketball star.
As that, he'd be famous!

14

If my pet dinosaur
stood very still,
he would look like a mountain
or maybe a hill.
I could slide down in springtime . . .

15

roll down in fall . . .

16

and ski down in winter!

But the best time of all
would be summer.

Imagine the thrill of a

cycle ride down a dinosaur hill!

19

How about a high dive
from a dinosaur's nose?
Or skin diving around
a dinosaur's toes?

If my dinosaur swam far out to sea,
he would look like an island!

Or he could be a ship!
I could rig up a sail
on the tip of his tail

and take a long trip
on my dinosaur ship.

We would sail to the park

where we'd play until dark.

In a kite-flying contest,
he would be best.
His kite would fly higher
than all the rest.

But I would beat him at "hide and seek",
even though I wouldn't peek.

If my dinosaur
came to dinner,
guess what I would do?

I would make delicious,
delicate doughnuts for him. . .

to dip in his dandelion stew!

Creative dramatics provides a framework for the expression of many emotions and thoughts. Children are constantly dramatizing events that have happened to them, characters and situations they have seen on television, and happenings people have discussed with them. Through imaginative play, a child restructures his own experiences and discovers new ones. By imitating others in play, he comes to understand what they do and why, and also how their actions affect him.

About the Author:

Jane Belk Moncure, author of many books and stories for young children, is a graduate of Virginia Commonwealth University and Columbia University. She has taught nursery, kindergarten and primary children in Europe and America. Mrs. Moncure has taught early childhood education while serving on the faculties of Virginia Commonwealth University and the University of Richmond. She was the first president of the Virginia Association for Early Childhood Education and has been recognized widely for her services to young children. She is married to Dr. James A. Moncure, Vice President of Elon College, and currently lives in Burlington, North Carolina.

About the Artist:

Helen Endres is a commercial artist, designer and illustrator of children's books. She has lived and worked in the Chicago area since coming from her native Oklahoma in 1952. Graduated from Tulsa University with a BA, she received further training at Hallmark in Kansas City and from the Chicago Art Institute. Ms. Endres attributes much of her creative achievement to the advice and encouragement of her Chicago contemporaries and to the good humor and patience of the hundreds of young models who have posed for her.